SLIM & HEALTHY COOKERY

This is not a cranky 'health food' book. It is a cookbook about sensible eating, about choosing and using the best ingredients to keep you and your family as healthy, slim and fit as possible. Food plays a vital part in determining our health, and much is talked about the importance of a well-balanced diet, low in fat and high in fibre. We show you how to cook interesting dishes which illustrate this point without trying to completely change your eating habits.

With the compliments of

COOKERY NOTES

Follow either metric or imperial measures for the recipes in this book as they are not interchangeable. Sets of spoon measures are available in both metric and imperial size to give accurate measurement of small quantities. All spoon measures are level unless otherwise stated. When measuring milk we have used the exact conversion of 568 ml (1 pint).

* Size 2 eggs should be used except when otherwise stated.
† Granulated sugar is used unless otherwise stated.
● Plain flour is used unless otherwise stated.

OVEN TEMPERATURE CHART

°C	°F	Gas mark
110	225	$\frac{1}{4}$
130	250	$\frac{1}{2}$
140	275	1
150	300	2
170	325	3
180	350	4
190	375	5
200	400	6
220	425	7
230	450	8
240	475	9

METRIC CONVERSION SCALE

LIQUID		
Imperial	Exact conversion	Recommended ml
$\frac{1}{4}$ pint	142 ml	150 ml
$\frac{1}{2}$ pint	284 ml	300 ml
1 pint	568 ml	600 ml
$1\frac{1}{2}$ pints	851 ml	900 ml
$1\frac{3}{4}$ pints	992 ml	1 litre

For quantities of $1\frac{3}{4}$ pints and over, litres and fractions of a litre have been used.

SOLID		
Imperial	Exact conversion	Recommended g
1 oz	28.35 g	25 g
2 oz	56.7 g	50 g
4 oz	113.4 g	100 g
8 oz	226.8 g	225 g
12 oz	340.2 g	350 g
14 oz	397.0 g	400 g
16 oz (1 lb)	453.6 g	450 g

1 kilogram (kg) equals 2.2 lb.

KEY TO SYMBOLS

$\boxed{1.00*}$ Indicates minimum preparation and cooking times in hours and minutes. They do not include prepared items in the list of ingredients; calculated times apply only to the method. An asterisk * indicates extra time should be allowed, so check the note below symbols.

⌂ Chef's hats indicate degree of difficulty of a recipe: no hat means it is straightforward; one hat slightly more complicated; two hats indicates that it is for more advanced cooks.

£ Indicates a recipe which is good value for money; £ £ indicates an expensive recipe. No £ sign indicates an inexpensive recipe.

✳ Indicates that a recipe will freeze. If there is no symbol, the recipe is unsuitable for freezing. An asterisk * indicates special freezer instructions so check the note immediately below the symbols.

$\boxed{309\ cals}$ Indicates calories per serving, including any suggestions (e.g. cream, to serve) given in the ingredients.

Illustrated on the cover: Fish Kebabs (page 36)

GOOD HOUSEKEEPING

SLIM & HEALTHY COOKERY

Contents

MUESLI

0.10	£	175 cals

Makes 14 servings

250 g (9 oz) porridge oats

75 g (3 oz) wholewheat flakes

50 g (2 oz) bran buds

75 g (3 oz) sunflower seeds

175 g (6 oz) sultanas

175 g (6 oz) dried pears (or apricots, figs or peaches), cut into small pieces

1 Mix together the porridge oats, wholewheat flakes, bran buds, sunflower seeds, sultanas and dried pears. (The dried fruits can be varied according to taste and availability, but keep the ratio of grains to fruit about the same.)

2 The dry muesli will keep fresh for several weeks if stored in an airtight container.

MUESLI

The original idea for muesli as a breakfast dish came from a Swiss doctor called Max Bircher-Benner, which is why some brands of muesli are called 'Bircher Muesli'. Dr Bircher-Benner had a clinic in Zurich at the beginning of the century, where he prescribed muesli for his patients, to be eaten both at breakfast time and supper. The original muesli was based on fresh fruit, with porridge oats (the German word *muesli* means gruel) added. This is why muesli cereal is usually eaten with fruit—in this recipe dried fruit is suggested, but fresh fruit may be used instead.

DRIED FRUIT COMPOTE

0.15*	£	80 cals

* plus overnight macerating

Serves 6

50 g (2 oz) dried apple rings
50 g (2 oz) dried apricots
50 g (2 oz) dried figs
300 ml (½ pint) unsweetened orange
   juice
300 ml (½ pint) water
25 g (1 oz) hazelnuts

1 Cut the dried apples, apricots and figs into chunky pieces and place in a bowl.

2 Mix together the unsweetened orange juice and water and pour over the fruit in the bowl. Cover and leave to macerate in the refrigerator overnight.

3 The next day, spread the hazelnuts out in a grill pan and toast under a low to moderate heat, shaking the pan frequently until the hazelnuts are browned evenly on all sides.

4 Tip the hazelnuts into a clean tea-towel and rub them while they are still hot to remove the skins.

5 Chop the hazelnuts roughly using an automatic chopper or large cook's knife. Sprinkle over the compote just before serving.

VEGETABLE VITALITY DRINK

0.40*	293 cals

* including 30 minutes infusing

Serves 1

50 g (2 oz) shredded coconut
300 ml (½ pint) boiling water
225 g (8 oz) carrots
juice of ½ lemon
5 ml (1 tsp) wheatgerm oil

1 Put the coconut in a heatproof jug, pour on the boiling water and stir well to mix. Leave to infuse for 30 minutes.

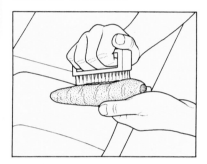

2 Meanwhile, scrub the carrots with a stiff vegetable brush to remove any soil from their skins. Grate into a blender or food processor, add the lemon juice and blend until the carrots are broken down to a pulp.

3 Strain the carrot pulp through a sieve into a jug, then strain in the milk from the coconut. Add the wheatgerm oil and whisk vigorously to combine. Pour into a long glass and serve immediately.

YOGURT VITALITY DRINK

0.05	280 cals

Serves 1

1 small banana
10 ml (2 tsp) wheatgerm
juice of 1 orange
150 ml (¼ pint) natural yogurt
1 egg yolk

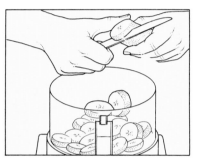

1 Peel the banana and slice straight into a blender or food processor.

2 Add the wheatgerm, orange juice, yogurt and egg yolk and blend to a smooth mixture. Pour into a long glass and serve immediately.

FRUITY VITALITY DRINK

0.05	195 cals

Serves 1

2 pink grapefruit
1 lemon
1 egg
10 ml (2 tsp) honey, or to taste
5 ml (1 tsp) wheatgerm

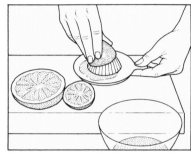

1 Squeeze the juice from the grapefruit and lemon, and pour into a blender or food processor.

2 Add the egg, honey and wheatgerm and blend until well combined. Taste for sweetness and add more honey if liked. Pour into a long glass and serve immediately.

CAULIFLOWER BUTTERMILK SOUP

| 0.50 | £ | 258 cals |

Serves 6

900 g (2 lb) cauliflower

1 large onion, skinned

50 g (2 oz) butter or margarine

1 garlic clove, skinned and crushed

15 ml (1 tbsp) plain flour

900 ml (1½ pints) milk

2 eggs, beaten

300 ml (½ pint) buttermilk

pinch of freshly grated nutmeg

salt and freshly ground pepper

25 g (1 oz) flaked almonds

15 ml (1 tbsp) chopped fresh parsley

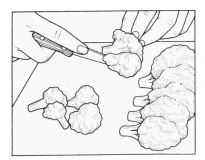

1 Cut away any green stalks from the cauliflower, and cut it into small florets. Roughly chop the onion.

2 Melt 25 g (1 oz) of the butter in a saucepan. Add the onion and garlic and fry for 3–4 minutes until golden.

3 Stir in the flour. Cook, stirring, for 1 minute, then add the milk and cauliflower.

4 Bring to the boil, cover and simmer for 25–30 minutes or until the cauliflower is very soft.

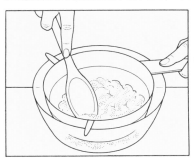

5 Work the soup to a very smooth purée in a blender or food processor, or rub through a sieve.

6 Return to the rinsed-out pan. Beat in the eggs, buttermilk, nutmeg and salt and pepper to taste. Reheat very gently, without boiling.

7 Melt the remaining butter in a small frying pan. Add the almonds and parsley and fry until the nuts are golden. Scatter over the soup before serving.

Menu Suggestion
Serve this creamy, nutritious soup for a quick lunch. Wholemeal baps and a selection of cheeses would go well with it.

SPICED DAL SOUP

1.30	£	123–185 cals

Serves 4–6

100 g (4 oz) channa dal
5 ml (1 tsp) cumin seeds
10 ml (2 tsp) coriander seeds
5 ml (1 tsp) fenugreek seeds
3 dried red chillies
15 ml (1 tbsp) shredded coconut
30 ml (2 tbsp) ghee or vegetable oil
225 g (8 oz) tomatoes, skinned and roughly chopped
2.5 ml ($\frac{1}{2}$ tsp) turmeric
15 ml (1 tbsp) lemon juice
5 ml (1 tsp) treacle
5 ml (1 tsp) salt
lemon slices and coriander sprigs, to garnish

1 Pick over the dal and remove any grit or discoloured pulses. Put into a sieve and wash thoroughly under cold running water. Drain well.

2 Place the dal in a large saucepan, cover with 600 ml (1 pint) water and bring to the boil. Cover and simmer for at least 1 hour, or until tender.

3 Finely grind the cumin, coriander, fenugreek, chillies and coconut in a small electric mill or with a pestle and mortar. Heat the ghee in a heavy-based frying pan, add the spice mixture and fry, stirring, for 30 seconds. Set the spices aside.

4 Mash or liquidise the dal and transfer to a large saucepan. Stir in the tomatoes, spices, turmeric, lemon juice, treacle, salt and a further 300 ml ($\frac{1}{2}$ pint) water.

5 Bring to the boil, then lower the heat, cover and simmer for about 20 minutes. Taste and adjust seasoning and turn into a warmed serving dish. Garnish with lemon slices and coriander sprigs and serve immediately.

SPICED DAL SOUP

The shredded coconut in this recipe can be fresh if you want to go to the trouble of preparing a fresh coconut, but for such a small quantity it is more practical to buy ready shredded coconut. It has larger flakes than desiccated coconut, and a fuller flavour. Toasted, it would make an attractive garnish for this soup.

LENTIL CROQUETTES

1.10* £ ✳* 183 cals

* plus 1 hour chilling; freeze after shaping in step 5

Makes 8

225 g (8 oz) split red lentils

2 celery sticks, trimmed and finely chopped

1 onion, skinned and chopped

1–2 garlic cloves, skinned and crushed

600 ml (1 pint) water

10 ml (2 tsp) garam masala

1 egg, beaten

salt and freshly ground pepper

30 ml (2 tbsp) wholewheat flour, to coat

5 ml (1 tsp) paprika

5 ml (1 tsp) ground turmeric

60 ml (4 tbsp) vegetable oil

fresh coriander or parsley and lime wedges, to garnish

1 Place the lentils in a large saucepan with the celery, onion, garlic, water and garam masala. Bring to the boil, stirring with a wooden spoon to mix.

2 Lower the heat and simmer gently for 30 minutes or until the lentils are tender and have absorbed all the liquid. Stir frequently to prevent the lentils sticking to the bottom of the pan.

3 Remove from the heat. Leave to cool for a few minutes, then beat in the egg and seasoning to taste.

4 Turn the mixture on to a board or flat plate and spread out evenly. Leave until cold, then chill in the refrigerator for 30 minutes to firm the mixture.

5 With floured hands, form the mixture into 8 triangular croquette shapes. Coat in the flour mixed with the paprika and turmeric. Chill again 30 minutes.

6 Heat the oil in a large frying pan, add the croquettes and fry over moderate to high heat for 10 minutes, turning once until crisp and golden on both sides.

7 Drain on absorbent kitchen paper and serve hot, with a sprinkling of chopped coriander or parsley on top of each and lime wedges.

BUTTER BEAN PÂTÉ

| 2.30* | £ | ✳ | 151–202 cals |

* plus overnight soaking
Serves 6–8

225 g (8 oz) dried butter beans,
 soaked in cold water overnight
60 ml (4 tbsp) olive oil
juice of 2 lemons
2 garlic cloves, skinned and
 crushed
30 ml (2 tbsp) chopped fresh
 coriander
salt and freshly ground pepper
coriander sprigs and black olives,
 to garnish

1 Drain the butter beans into a
 sieve and rinse thoroughly
under cold running water. Put in a
saucepan, cover with cold water
and bring to the boil.

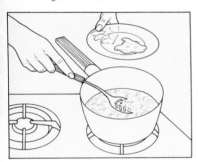

2 With a slotted spoon, skim off
 any scum that rises to the
surface. Half cover the pan with a
lid and simmer for 1½–2 hours
until the beans are very tender.

3 Drain the beans and rinse
 under cold running water. Put
half of the beans in a blender or
food processor with half of the oil,
lemon juice, garlic and coriander.
Blend to a smooth purée, then
transfer to a bowl. Repeat with the
remaining beans, oil, lemon juice,
garlic and coriander.

4 Beat the 2 batches of purée
 together until well mixed, then
add seasoning to taste.

5 Turn the pâté into a serving
 bowl and rough up the surface
with the prongs of a fork. Garnish
with the coriander and black
olives. Chill in the refrigerator
until serving time.

—— VARIATION ——

If you want to make this dip really
quickly, use two 396 g (14 oz) cans
butter beans and start the recipe
from the beginning of step 3.

BAKED POTATOES WITH CHICK PEAS

| *1.50* | £ | 492 cals |

Serves 4

4 baking potatoes, each
  weighing about 275 g (10 oz)

45 ml (3 tbsp) vegetable oil

salt and freshly ground pepper

1 medium onion, skinned and
  roughly chopped

2.5 ml ($\frac{1}{2}$ tsp) ground coriander

2.5 ml ($\frac{1}{2}$ tsp) ground cumin

400 g (14 oz) can chick peas, drained

60 ml (4 tbsp) chopped fresh
  parsley

150 ml ($\frac{1}{4}$ pint) natural yogurt

chopped fresh parsley, to garnish

1 Scrub the potatoes and pat dry. Brush them with 15 ml (1 tbsp) of the vegetable oil and sprinkle lightly with salt.

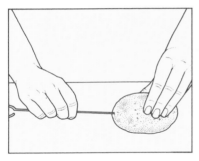

2 Run thin skewers through the potatoes to help conduct the heat through them. Place them directly on the oven shelves and bake in the oven at 200°C (400°F) mark 6 for 1$\frac{1}{4}$ hours until tender.

3 Meanwhile, heat remaining oil in a large saucepan, add the onion, coriander and cumin and fry for 4 minutes, stirring occasionally. Add the chick peas and cook for a further 1–2 minutes, stirring all the time.

4 Halve the potatoes and scoop out the flesh, keeping the shells intact. Add the potato flesh to the chick pea mixture with the parsley and yogurt. Mash until smooth; add seasoning to taste.

5 Place the potato shells on a baking sheet and fill with the potato and chick pea mixture. Return to the oven and bake for a further 10–15 minutes. Serve hot sprinkled with chopped parsley.

CRUNCHY BAKED POTATO SKINS

| *1.40* | £ | 198 cals |

Serves 4

4 medium baking potatoes
60 ml (4 tbsp) vegetable oil
salt and freshly ground pepper
300 ml ($\frac{1}{2}$ pint) natural yogurt
30 ml (2 tbsp) snipped chives

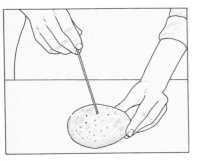

1 Pierce the potatoes all over with a skewer, then place directly on the oven shelf. Bake in the oven at 200°C (400°F) mark 6 for 1$\frac{1}{4}$ hours until tender.

2 Cut each potato in half lengthways and scoop out most of the flesh with a sharp-edged teaspoon, taking care not to split the skins.

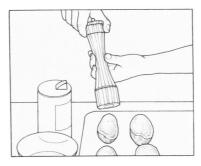

3 Stand the potato skins on a lightly oiled baking sheet. Brush them inside and out with the oil and sprinkle with plenty of salt and freshly ground pepper.

4 Increase the oven temperature to 220°C (425°F) mark 7 and bake for 10 minutes until crisp.

5 Meanwhile, whisk the yogurt and chives together with seasoning to taste. Spoon into a serving bowl or sauceboat.

6 Serve the potato skins piping hot, with the yogurt dressing handed separately.

SPINACH ROULADE

1.00	🍴	352 cals

Serves 3–4

900 g (2 lb) spinach, trimmed, or 450 g (1 lb) packet frozen spinach
4 eggs, size 2, separated
pinch of freshly grated nutmeg
salt and freshly ground pepper
25 g (1 oz) butter or margarine
1 medium onion, skinned and finely chopped
100 g (4 oz) curd cheese
50 g (2 oz) Gruyère cheese, grated
30 ml (2 tbsp) soured cream

1 Grease a 35.5 × 25.5 cm (14 × 10 inch) Swiss roll tin and line with non-stick baking parchment. Set aside.

2 Wash the fresh spinach in several changes of cold water. Place in a saucepan with only the water that clings to the leaves. Cook gently, covered, for about 5 minutes until wilted or until thawed, about 7–10 minutes, if using frozen spinach.

3 Drain the spinach well and chop finely. Turn into a bowl and allow to cool slightly for about 5 minutes, then beat in the egg yolks, nutmeg and salt and pepper to taste.

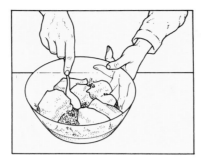

4 Whisk the egg whites until they form stiff peaks, then fold into the spinach mixture with a large metal spoon until they are evenly incorporated.

5 Spread the mixture in the prepared tin. Bake in the oven at 200°C (400°F) mark 6 for 15–20 minutes, until firm.

6 Meanwhile, prepare the filling. Melt the butter in a saucepan. Add the onion and fry gently for about 5 minutes until soft and lightly coloured. Remove from the heat and stir in the cheeses, soured cream and salt and pepper to taste.

7 Turn the roulade out on to greaseproof paper, peel off the lining paper and spread the roulade immediately and quickly with the cheese mixture.

8 Roll the roulade up by gently lifting the greasproof paper. Serve hot, cut into thick slices.

SPINACH ROULADE

The curd cheese used in the filling of this roulade is a medium fat soft cheese made from semi-skimmed milk. It is naturally soured, without the addition of rennet. It has a good, firm texture, ideal for a filling such as this roulade which has to keep its shape when rolled up. Cream cheese or full fat soft cheese has a similar texture and could be used instead but it is much fattier so best avoided. Many super-markets and delicatessens now sell continental-type soft cheeses in small tubs or cartons. Called 'quark', 'fromage frais' and 'fromage blanc', these are low in fat and excellent.

WHOLEWHEAT SPINACH PANCAKES

| 0.40 | ✳* | 313 cals |

* freeze pancakes only at the end of step 7

Serves 4

175 g (6 oz) fresh spinach, washed
100 g (4 oz) wholewheat flour
salt and freshly ground pepper
150 ml ($\frac{1}{4}$ pint) milk
150 ml ($\frac{1}{4}$ pint) water
1 egg, beaten
about 45 ml (3 tbsp) vegetable oil, for frying
225 g (8 oz) cottage cheese with prawns
2.5 ml ($\frac{1}{2}$ tsp) paprika
whole prawns and sprigs of herbs, to garnish

1 Cut away the thick midribs and stalks from the spinach and put the leaves in a saucepan with only the water that clings to them. Cover and cook gently for 5 minutes until tender.

2 Drain the spinach in a colander, pressing down with a spoon to extract as much water as possible from the leaves.

3 Turn the spinach on to a board and chop very finely with a sharp knife.

4 Put the flour in a bowl with a pinch of salt. Make a well in the centre, add half of the milk and water and the egg.

5 Beat vigorously with a whisk, gradually incorporating the flour into the centre. Whisk in the remaining liquid and the spinach.

6 Heat a little oil in a pancake pan or heavy-based 18 cm (7 inch) frying pan. Pour the batter into a jug and whisk.

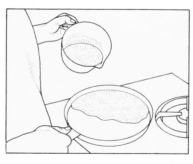

7 Pour one-eighth of the batter into the pan and tip and tilt the pan so that the batter runs all over the base. Cook over moderate heat for about 30 seconds until the underside is golden, then turn the pancake over and repeat cooking on the other side.

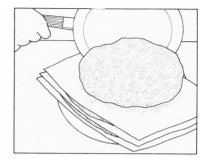

8 Slide the pancake out on to a sheet of greaseproof paper placed over a plate and keep warm while cooking the remaining 7 pancakes. (As each pancake is made, stack it on top of the last one, with greaseproof in between.)

9 Season the cottage cheese with the paprika and salt and pepper to taste. Spread a little over each pancake, then roll up or fold into parcels. Serve immediately garnished with the prawns and herbs.

PEPPER AND TOMATO OMELETTE

| 0.20 | £ | 490 cals |

Serves 2

30 ml (2 tbsp) olive oil

1 onion, skinned and sliced

2 garlic cloves, skinned and crushed

1 green pepper, cored, seeded and sliced

1 red pepper, cored, seeded and sliced

4 tomatoes, skinned and sliced

5 eggs

pinch of dried mixed herbs, or to taste

salt and freshly ground pepper

50 g (2 oz) hard mature cheese (eg Parmesan, Farmhouse Cheddar), grated

1 Heat the olive oil in a non-stick frying pan. Add the onion and garlic and fry gently for 5 minutes until soft.

2 Add the pepper slices and the tomatoes and fry for a further 2–3 minutes, stirring frequently.

3 In a jug, beat the eggs lightly with the herbs and seasoning to taste. Pour into the pan, allowing the egg to run to the sides.

4 Draw in the vegetable mixture with a palette knife so that the mixture runs on to the base of the pan. Cook over moderate heat for 5 minutes until the underside of the omelette is set.

5 Sprinkle the top of the omelette with the grated cheese, then put under a pre-heated hot grill for 2–3 minutes until set and browned. Slide onto a serving plate and cut into wedges to serve.

PEPPER AND TOMATO OMELETTE

This type of omelette is different from the classic French kind, which is cooked for a very short time and served folded over. Pepper and Tomato Omelette is more like the Spanish tortilla, a flat omelette which is cooked for a fairly long time so that the eggs become quite set, then browned under a hot grill so that both sides become firm. Some Spanish cooks turn their tortilla several times during cooking, and there is even a special kind of plate used in Spain which is designed to make the turning easier. Take care when making this kind of omelette that the frying pan you use is not too heavy to lift when you are transferring it to finish off the cooking under the grill. Light, non-stick frying pans are better than the traditional cast iron ones.

WHOLEWHEAT MACARONI BAKE

| 0.50 | £ ✳* | 273–410 cals |

* freeze at the end of step 7

Serves 4–6

175 g (6 oz) wholewheat macaroni

salt and freshly ground pepper

30 ml (2 tbsp) vegetable oil

1 onion, skinned and chopped

225 g (8 oz) button mushrooms, wiped

350 g (12 oz) tomatoes, skinned and roughly chopped

300 ml (½ pint) vegetable stock

15 ml (1 tbsp) tomato purée

5 ml (1 tsp) dried mixed herbs

5 ml (1 tsp) dried oregano

30 ml (2 tbsp) wholewheat flour

300 ml (½ pint) milk

100 g (4 oz) low-fat soft cheese

1 egg, beaten

5 ml (1 tsp) English mustard powder

30 ml (2 tbsp) wholewheat breadcrumbs

30 ml (2 tbsp) grated Parmesan cheese

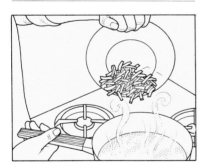

1 Plunge the macaroni into a large saucepan of boiling salted water. Simmer, uncovered, for 10 minutes.

2 Meanwhile, heat the oil in a separate pan, add the onion and fry gently for 5 minutes until soft but not coloured.

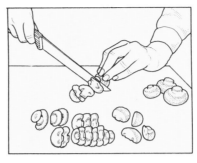

3 Cut the small mushrooms in half, slice the larger ones. Add to the pan, increase the heat and toss with the onion for 1–2 minutes until the juices run.

4 Add the tomatoes and stock and bring to the boil, stirring constantly to break up the tomatoes. Lower the heat, add the tomato purée, herbs and seasoning to taste, and simmer gently for 10 minutes.

5 Drain the macaroni into a colander and leave to stand while making the cheese sauce.

6 Put the flour and milk in a blender or food processor and blend for 1 minute. Transfer to a heavy-based pan and simmer, stirring constantly, for 5 minutes until thickened. Remove from the heat and beat in the cheese, egg, mustard and seasoning to taste.

7 Mix the macaroni with the mushrooms in tomato sauce, then pour into a baking dish. Pour the cheese sauce over the top and sprinkle with the breadcrumbs and Parmesan.

8 Bake in the oven at 190°C (375°F) mark 5 for 20 minutes until golden brown and bubbling. Serve hot, straight from the dish.

WHOLEWHEAT MACARONI BAKE

Wholewheat macaroni is now widely available from supermarkets and health food shops. It is made from 100 per cent wholewheat flour and therefore has more fibre than ordinary white varieties. The flavour of wholewheat macaroni is pleasantly nutty and the texture quite firm—check with packet instructions for exact cooking times of each brand, because many of them tend to be longer than for white pasta. In Italy, wholewheat pasta is rarely seen and the short-cut or elbow macaroni that we are used to is not so common. Italian *maccheroni* tubes vary in length and thickness from one manufacturer to another. Other types of Italian pasta similar to *maccheroni* which you may see in the shops are *penne* and *rigatoni*.

PAPRIKA BEEF

| 2.15 | £ | ✳ | 213 cals |

Serves 4

450 g (1 lb) lean shin of beef

15 ml (1 tbsp) plain wholewheat flour

7.5 ml (1½ tsp) mild paprika

1.25 ml (¼ tsp) caraway seeds

1.25 ml (¼ tsp) dried marjoram

salt and freshly ground pepper

175 g (6 oz) onion, skinned and sliced

225 g (8 oz) carrots, peeled and sliced

200 ml (7 fl oz) beef stock

15 ml (1 tbsp) tomato purée

1 garlic clove, skinned and crushed

1 whole clove

100 g (4 oz) button mushrooms, wiped and sliced

chopped fresh parsley, to garnish

1 Trim the fat from the beef. Cut the meat into chunky cubes. Mix together the flour, paprika, caraway seeds, marjoram and seasoning to taste. Toss the beef in the seasoned flour.

2 Layer the meat, onion and carrots in a 2 litre (3½ pint) flameproof casserole.

3 Whisk together the stock, tomato purée, crushed garlic and clove. Pour into the casserole. Bring to the boil and simmer, uncovered, for 3–4 minutes.

4 Cover the casserole tightly and cook in the oven at 180°C (350°F) mark 4 for about 1½ hours, stirring occasionally.

5 Remove the casserole from the oven and stir in the mushrooms. Cover again and return to the oven for a further 15 minutes or until the meat is tender. Taste and adjust seasoning. Garnish.

APPLE BAKED CHOPS

| 1.30 | ✳ | 299 cals |

Serves 4

225 g (8 oz) dessert apples

75 g (3 oz) onion, skinned

50 g (2 oz) raisins

200 ml (7 fl oz) unsweetened apple juice

45 ml (3 tbsp) chopped parsley

salt and freshly ground pepper

4 pork loin chops, about 175 g (6 oz) each, trimmed of fat

3 or 4 green cardamoms, lightly crushed

30 ml (2 tbsp) dry white wine or cider

parsley sprigs, to garnish

1 Core and finely chop the apple. Finely chop the onion. Place in a saucepan with the raisins and apple juice. Simmer gently, uncovered, for 3–4 minutes until the apple begins to soften slightly.

2 Remove from the heat, drain off the juices and reserve. Stir the parsley into the apple mixture with seasoning to taste, then cool.

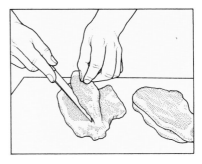

3 Meanwhile, make a horizontal cut through the flesh of the chops, almost to the bone. Open out to form a pocket for the apple.

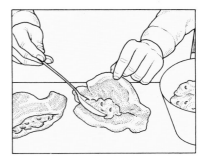

4 Spoon a little of the apple mixture into the pocket of each chop. Place in a shallow flame-proof dish. Sprinkle any remaining stuffing around the chops, with the crushed cardamoms. Mix the reserved juices with the wine or cider and pour over the chops.

5 Cover with foil and bake in the oven at 190°C (375°F) mark 5 for about 1 hour until tender.

6 Remove the chops from the dish and place in a grill pan. Grill until browned.

7 Meanwhile, pour the cooking juices from the chops into a pan and boil rapidly until reduced by half. Arrange the chops on a dish and pour over the reduced juices. Garnish with parsley.

LAMB CUTLETS WITH LEMON AND GARLIC

| 0.35 | £ £ | 502 cals |

Serves 4

2 lemons

3 small garlic cloves, skinned and
  crushed

salt and freshly ground pepper

8 lamb cutlets

30 ml (2 tbsp) vegetable oil

25 g (1 oz) margarine or butter

1 medium onion, skinned and
  finely chopped

175 ml (6 fl oz) natural yogurt

150 ml ($\frac{1}{4}$ pint) chicken stock

5 ml (1 tsp) chopped fresh basil or
  2.5 ml ($\frac{1}{2}$ tsp) dried

parsley or basil sprigs, to garnish

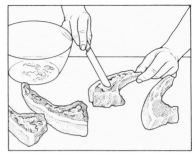

1 On the finest side of a conical or box grater, grate the rind of 1$\frac{1}{2}$ lemons into a bowl. Add the garlic and freshly ground pepper to taste and blend together.

2 Place the cutlets on a board and spread the lemon rind and garlic evenly over the meat. Leave for 15 minutes.

3 Heat the oil and margarine in a pan, add the cutlets and fry for about 3 minutes each side or until tender. Drain and keep warm on a serving dish.

4 Pour off all but 30 ml (2 tbsp) fat from the pan, add the onion and fry gently for 5 minutes until soft but not coloured. Stir in the yogurt and stock with the squeezed juice of the 1$\frac{1}{2}$ lemons and the basil. Bring to the boil and simmer for 2–3 minutes. Add salt and freshly ground pepper to taste.

5 Spoon the juices over the meat and garnish with the parsley or basil sprigs and the remaining $\frac{1}{2}$ lemon, cut into wedges, if liked. Serve immediately.

MINTED LAMB MEATBALLS

| 1.20 | £ | 201 cals |

Serves 4

225 g (8 oz) crisp cabbage, trimmed and finely chopped

450 g (1 lb) lean minced lamb

100 g (4 oz) onion, skinned and finely chopped

2.5 ml ($\frac{1}{2}$ tsp) ground allspice

salt and freshly ground pepper

397 g (14 oz) can tomato juice

1 bay leaf

10 ml (2 tsp) chopped fresh mint or 5 ml (1 tsp) dried

15 ml (1 tbsp) chopped fresh parsley

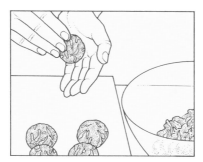

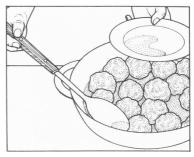

1 Steam the cabbage for 2–3 minutes or until softened.

2 Place the lamb and cabbage in a bowl with the onion, allspice and seasoning to taste. Beat well to combine all the ingredients.

3 With your hands, shape the mixture into 16–20 small balls. Place the meatballs in a shallow large ovenproof dish.

4 Mix the tomato juice with the bay leaf, mint and parsley. Pour over the meatballs. Cover the dish tightly and bake in the oven at 180°C (350°F) mark 4 for about 1 hour until the meatballs are cooked.

5 Skim any fat off the tomato sauce before serving, and taste and adjust seasoning. Serve hot.

TANDOORI CHICKEN

1.40*	✳*	315 cals

* plus 24 hours marinating; freeze in
the marinade

Serves 4

**4 large chicken portions, each
weighing about 10 oz (275 g)**
30 ml (2 tbsp) lime or lemon juice
**2 garlic cloves, skinned and
crushed**
5 ml (1 tsp) chilli powder
salt and freshly ground pepper
15 ml (1 tbsp) cumin seeds
15 ml (1 tbsp) coriander seeds
**2.5 cm (1 inch) piece of fresh root
ginger, peeled and chopped**
60 ml (4 tbsp) natural yogurt
10 ml (2 tsp) garam masala
**2.5 ml ($\frac{1}{2}$ tsp) red or orange food
colouring**
**50 ml (2 fl oz) ghee or melted
butter**
**shredded lettuce, onion rings and
lemon wedges, to serve**

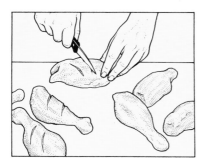

1 Cut each chicken portion in
half and remove the skin.
Slash each piece of chicken in
several places with a sharp,
pointed knife.

2 In a bowl, mix together the
lime or lemon juice, garlic,
chilli powder, 5 ml (1 tsp) salt and
plenty of pepper. Rub all over the
chicken, then place in a single
layer in a shallow dish. Set aside
while preparing the remaining
ingredients.

3 Grind the cumin and
coriander seeds and the ginger
in a small electric mill or with a
pestle and mortar. Turn into a
bowl and mix in the yogurt, garam
masala and food colouring.

4 Brush the marinade all over
the chicken, working it into
the cuts in the flesh. Cover the
dish and marinate in the
refrigerator for 24 hours.

5 When ready to cook, place the
chicken pieces on a rack in a
roasting tin. Pour enough water
under the rack to just cover the
bottom of the tin. Brush the ghee
or butter over the chicken, then
roast in the oven at 200°C (400°F)
mark 6 for 1 hour, turning once
and basting with the liquid from
the bottom of the tin.

6 To serve, arrange the lettuce
and onion rings on a large
platter. Place the chicken on top,
then garnish with lemon wedges.
Serve hot.

TANDOORI CHICKEN
Small tandoori ovens are sold
at specialist kitchen shops, but
even if you invest in one, it is
unlikely that you will achieve the
same colour and flavour that
come from the traditional clay
oven used in Indian restaurants.
This recipe works very well in a
conventional oven, but if you
prefer the chicken pieces to have
the charred appearance of
authentic tandoori, cook them on
a barbecue.

HINDLE WAKES

3.15*	£	281–421 cals

* plus overnight soaking

Serves 4–6

1.6 kg (3½ lb) boiling chicken with giblets, trussed

600 ml (1 pint) water

salt and freshly ground pepper

50 g (2 oz) butter or margarine

450 g (1 lb) leeks, sliced and washed

6 carrots, peeled and thickly sliced

225 g (8 oz) prunes, soaked overnight and stoned

25 g (1 oz) plain flour

1 Place the giblets in a saucepan with the water and 5 ml (1 tsp) salt. Bring to the boil, then cover and simmer for 30 minutes.

2 Meanwhile, melt 25 g (1 oz) of the fat in a large flame-proof casserole and fry the chicken for about 8 minutes until browned all over. Remove from casserole.

3 Fry the leeks and carrots for 3 minutes. Return the chicken and add the drained prunes. Strain in the giblet stock and season with pepper.

4 Cover and cook in the oven at 170°C (325°F) mark 3 for about 2–2½ hours or until tender.

5 Arrange the chicken, vegetables and prunes on a large warmed platter. Keep hot.

6 Skim any fat off the sauce. Blend together the remaining fat and the flour to form a paste. Add to the sauce, a little at a time, and stir over a gentle heat until thickened. Do not boil. Adjust the seasoning to taste and serve the sauce separately.

QUICK TURKEY CURRY

| 0.45 | ✳ | 288–433 cals |

Serves 4–6

30 ml (2 tbsp) vegetable oil

3 bay leaves

2 cardamom pods, crushed

1 cinnamon stick, broken into
   short lengths

1 medium onion, skinned and
   thinly sliced

1 green pepper, cored, seeded and
   chopped (optional)

10 ml (2 tsp) paprika

7.5 ml (1½ tsp) garam masala

2.5 ml (½ tsp) turmeric

2.5 ml (½ tsp) chilli powder

salt and freshly-ground pepper

50 g (2 oz) unsalted cashew nuts

700 g (1½ lb) turkey fillets, skinned
   and cut into bite-size pieces

2 medium potatoes, blanched,
   peeled and cut into chunks

4 tomatoes, skinned and chopped,
   or 225-g (8-oz) can tomatoes

bay leaves, to garnish

1 Heat the oil in a flameproof casserole, add the bay leaves, cardamom and cinnamon and fry over moderate heat for 1–2 minutes. Add the onion and green pepper (if using), with the spices and salt and pepper to taste. Pour in enough water to moisten, then stir to mix for 1 minute.

2 Add the cashews and turkey, cover and simmer for 20 minutes. Turn the turkey occasionally during this time to ensure even cooking.

3 Add the potatoes and tomatoes and continue cooking a further 20 minutes until the turkey and potatoes are tender. Taste and adjust seasoning before serving. Garnish with bay leaves.

QUICK TURKEY CURRY

The subtle blend of spices gives this a medium hot taste, without being too fiery! Chilli powder should be used with caution, since it is intensely hot.

Garam masala is readily available from Indian shops, specialist stores and some supermarkets. However, if you'd like to make your own, you will need about 100 g (4 oz) mixed large and small green cardamoms, 50 g (2 oz) cumin seeds, 15 g (½ oz) each black peppercorns, cloves and stick cinnamon and a little grated nutmeg. Dry-fry the whole spices for a few minutes, then grind together, mix in the nutmeg and store in an airtight container.

KIDNEYS PROVENÇAL

0.35	211 cals

Serves 4

12–16 lambs' kidneys

30 ml (2 tbsp) olive oil

1 large onion, skinned and chopped

1–2 garlic cloves, skinned and crushed

3 medium courgettes, trimmed and sliced

4 large tomatoes, skinned and roughly chopped

100 ml (4 fl oz) red wine or stock

10 ml (2 tsp) chopped fresh basil or 5 ml (1 tsp) dried basil

salt and freshly ground pepper

12 black olives

sprigs of chervil, to garnish

4 Add the courgettes, tomatoes and wine or stock and bring to the boil, stirring constantly. Lower the heat and add half the basil with seasoning to taste. Simmer gently for 8 minutes until the kidneys are tender.

5 Add the olives to the pan and heat through for 1–2 minutes. Taste and adjust the seasoning. Sprinkle with the remaining basil and chervil just before serving. Serve very hot.

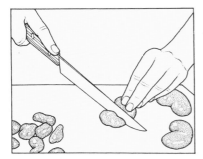

1 Skin the kidneys, then cut each one in half. Snip out the cores with kitchen scissors. Cut each half into two.

2 Heat the oil in a large heavy-based frying pan, add the onion and garlic to the pan and fry gently for 5 minutes until soft but not coloured.

3 Add the kidneys and fry over low heat for 3 minutes until they change colour. Shake the pan and toss the kidneys frequently during frying.

LIVER WITH VERMOUTH

| 0.35 | £ | 319 cals |

Serves 4

450 g (1 lb) lamb's liver, sliced

15 ml (1 tbsp) wholewheat flour

30 ml (2 tbsp) vegetable oil

1 onion, skinned and chopped

1 garlic clove, skinned and crushed

finely grated rind and juice of 1 orange

finely grated rind and juice of 1 lemon

60 ml (4 tbsp) sweet vermouth or sherry

30 ml (2 tbsp) chopped fresh parsley

salt and freshly ground pepper

few orange and lemon slices, to garnish

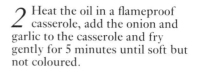

1 Cut the liver into thin strips, trimming away all ducts and gristle. Coat in the flour.

2 Heat the oil in a flameproof casserole, add the onion and garlic to the casserole and fry gently for 5 minutes until soft but not coloured.

3 Add the liver strips and cook over high heat until browned on all sides.

4 Add the orange and lemon rind and juices and the vermouth and bring to the boil. Stir constantly with a wooden spoon to scrape up any sediment and juices from the base of the casserole, and continue boiling until the sauce reduces.

5 Lower the heat and add half the parsley and salt and freshly ground pepper to taste.

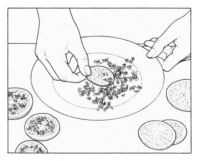

6 Dip the orange and lemon slices in the remaining chopped parsley. Transfer the liver and sauce to a warmed serving dish. Garnish with the orange and lemon slices and serve immediately, while piping hot.

STUFFED PLAICE FILLETS WITH MUSHROOM SAUCE

| 1.10 | 🍴 | 185 cals |

Serves 4

4 double plaice fillets

salt and freshly ground pepper

225 g (8 oz) cottage cheese with prawns (see box)

1.25 ml ($\frac{1}{4}$ tsp) Tabasco sauce, or less according to taste

finely grated rind and juice of 1 lemon

225 g (8 oz) button mushrooms, wiped and thinly sliced

90 ml (6 tbsp) dry white wine

5 ml (1 tsp) chopped fresh tarragon or dill or 2.5 ml ($\frac{1}{2}$ tsp) dried

8 unshelled prawns and fresh tarragon or dill sprigs, to garnish

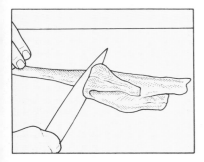

1 Skin the plaice fillets. Lay them flat, skin side down, on a board or work surface. Dip your fingers in salt and grip the tail end, then separate the flesh from the skin at this point with a sharp knife. Work the knife slowly between the skin and flesh using a sawing action until the opposite end of the fillet is reached. Cut each fillet into two lengthways.

2 Drain off any liquid from the cottage cheese, then mash the cheese with half of the Tabasco sauce, the grated lemon rind and seasoning to taste.

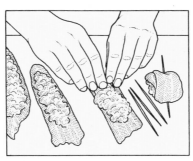

3 Lay the plaice fillets flat, with their skinned side facing upwards. Divide the cheese filling equally between them, then roll up and secure with wooden cocktail sticks, if necessary.

4 Place the stuffed fish rolls close together in a single layer in a lightly oiled ovenproof dish. Sprinkle the mushrooms around the fish, then pour over the wine mixed with the lemon juice and remaining Tabasco. Sprinkle with seasoning to taste.

5 Cover the dish with foil and cook in the oven at 180°C (350°F) mark 4 for 20 minutes or until the fish is just tender.

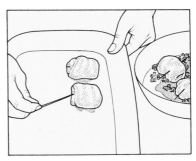

6 Remove the rolls from the liquid and discard the cocktail sticks. Arrange the fish on a warmed serving dish, cover loosely with foil and keep warm in the oven turned to its lowest setting.

7 Put the cooked mushrooms in a blender or food processor. Add the tarragon or dill and blend until smooth. Pour into a pan and heat through. Taste and adjust seasoning.

8 Pour a little sauce over each plaice roll, then top with a prawn and a tarragon or dill sprig. Serve immediately, with any remaining sauce handed separately in a jug.

STUFFED PLAICE FILLETS WITH MUSHROOM SAUCE

The cottage cheese with prawns used in the stuffing for these plaice fillets is available in cartons from selected super-markets. Look for a good-quality brand which is thick and firm-textured. Some brands of cottage cheese are watery and will not be suitable for this dish. If there is a little water on the surface of the cheese when you open the carton, be sure to drain it off before use.

MACKEREL PARCELS

| 1.00 | £ | 319 cals |

Serves 4

4 fresh mackerel, weighing about 175 g (6 oz) each

about 25 g (1 oz) margarine or butter

½ large cucumber

60 ml (4 tbsp) white wine vinegar

30 ml (2 tbsp) chopped fresh mint

5 ml (1 tsp) sugar

salt and freshly ground pepper

natural yogurt and chopped fresh mint, to serve

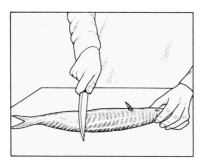

1 With the back of a knife and working from the tail towards the head, scrape off the scales from the skin of the mackerel.

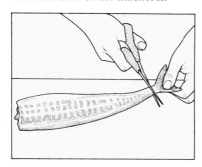

2 Cut off the heads just below the gills with a sharp knife. Cut off the fins and tails with kitchen scissors.

3 Slit the underside of the fish open from head to tail end with a sharp knife or scissors.

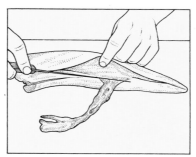

4 With the flat of the knife blade, scrape out the entrails of the fish, together with any membranes and blood. Wash the fish thoroughly inside and out under cold running water.

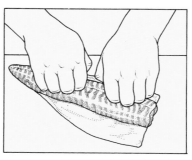

5 Lay the fish flat on a board or work surface with the skin uppermost. Press firmly along the backbone with your knuckles (this flattens the fish and loosens the backbone).

6 Turn the fish over and lift out the backbone with the help of a knife. Cut each fish lengthways into 2 fillets. Dry thoroughly with absorbent kitchen paper.

7 Brush 8 squares of kitchen foil with a little margarine. Put a mackerel fillet in the centre of each square, skin side down.

8 Arrange the cucumber slices on one half of the mackerel fillets, then sprinkle with the vinegar, mint, sugar and seasoning to taste. Dot with the remaining margarine in tiny pieces.

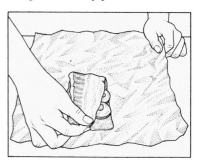

9 Fold the mackerel fillets over to enclose the cucumber filling, then wrap in the foil. Place the foil parcels in a single layer in an ovenproof dish. Cook in the oven at 200°C (400°F) mark 6 for 30 minutes until the fish is tender.

10 To serve, unwrap the foil parcels and carefully place the mackerel fillets in a circle on a warmed platter. Spoon yogurt in the centre and sprinkle with mint.

MACKEREL PARCELS

Fresh mackerel, like herring, are an inexpensive yet much neglected fish. And yet they are a good source of first-class protein, plus the minerals calcium and phosphorus which are essential for healthy bones. Mackerel flesh is also rich in vitamins A and D, so it makes sense to include it regularly in a healthy diet. Always make sure to cook mackerel on the day of purchase as it quickly deteriorates after catching.

FISH KEBABS

| 0.20* | 187 cals |

* plus 2 hours marinating

Serves 4

700 g (1½ lb) monkfish fillets, skinned

60 ml (4 tbsp) sunflower oil

juice of 2 limes or 1 lemon

1 small onion, skinned and roughly chopped

2 garlic cloves, skinned and crushed

2.5 ml (½ tsp) fennel seed

2.5 ml (½ tsp) dried thyme

freshly ground pepper

1 green pepper, halved, cored and seeded

16 whole cherry tomatoes or 4 small tomatoes, quartered

8 bay leaves

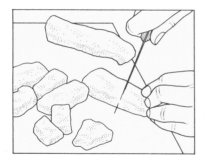

1 Cut the monkfish into 4 cm (1½ inch) chunks. Place the oil, lime or lemon juice, onion, garlic, fennel, thyme and pepper in a blender or food processor and blend until smooth. Toss the fish in this mixture, cover and marinate for at least 2 hours.

2 Meanwhile, place the green pepper in a saucepan of cold water and bring to the boil. Drain and cut into 12 pieces.

3 Thread the fish, green pepper, tomatoes and bay leaves on to 4 oiled skewers. Reserve the marinade for basting.

4 Cook the kebabs under a pre-heated moderate grill for about 10 minutes, basting with the marinade and turning once.

FISH KEBABS

In summertime, these kebabs would be excellent cooked on the barbecue—the additional flavour of the charcoal goes well with quick-cooking fish, and they would make an unusual alternative to steaks, chicken and chops. Follow the recipe exactly as above and make sure the barbecue coals are hot before cooking—they should look grey in daylight, glowing red at night. Food, especially delicately textured fish, should never be put over coals that are flaming, so wait for all flames to die down before starting to cook. Oil the barbecue grid well before placing the kebabs over the fire.

BUCKWHEAT AND LENTIL CASSEROLE

1.45	453 cals

Serves 4

450 ml (¾ pint) water

salt and freshly ground pepper

150 g (5 oz) buckwheat

30 ml (2 tbsp) vegetable oil

1 red or green pepper, cored, seeded and cut into strips

1 onion, skinned and finely chopped

350 g (12 oz) courgettes, trimmed and sliced

175 g (6 oz) mushrooms, sliced

225 g (8 oz) red lentils

3 bay leaves

30 ml (2 tbsp) lemon juice

1 garlic clove, skinned and crushed

2 rosemary sprigs

5 ml (1 tsp) cumin seeds

600 ml (1 pint) vegetable stock

25 g (1 oz) butter or margarine

chopped fresh parsley, to garnish

1 Bring the water to the boil in a saucepan, add a pinch of salt, then sprinkle in the buckwheat and return to the boil. Boil rapidly for 1 minute. Reduce the heat, cover and cook gently for 12 minutes or until the water has been absorbed. Do not stir. Transfer to a buttered casserole.

2 Heat the oil in a flameproof casserole and fry the pepper and onion for 5 minutes. Add the courgettes and mushrooms and fry for 5 minutes. Stir in the lentils, bay leaves, lemon juice, garlic, rosemary, cumin and stock. Add to the casserole and stir well.

3 Simmer for about 45 minutes until the lentils are cooked, stirring occasionally. Add the butter, adjust the seasoning and sprinkle with parsley. Serve hot with a bowl of grated cheese, if liked.

VEGETABLE HOT POT

| 1.30 | £ ✳ | 533 cals |

Serves 4

450 g (1 lb) carrots, peeled and thinly sliced

2 large onions, skinned and thinly sliced

3 celery sticks, trimmed and thinly sliced

450 g (1 lb) potatoes, peeled and sliced

100 g (4 oz) swede, peeled and thinly sliced

450 ml ($\frac{3}{4}$ pint) vegetable stock

bouquet garni

salt and freshly ground pepper

425 g (15 oz) can butter beans, drained

100 g (4 oz) frozen peas

175 g (6 oz) fresh breadcrumbs

175 g (6 oz) hard cheese, grated

1 Layer the carrot, onion, celery, potato and swede in a 2.3 litre (4 pint) casserole.

2 Pour the vegetable stock into the casserole and add the bouquet garni and seasoning.

3 Cover and cook the stock and vegetables in the oven at 180°C (350°F) mark 4 for 1 hour.

4 Remove the bouquet garni. Add the beans and peas to the casserole. Mix the breadcrumbs and cheese together. Spoon over the hot pot. Return to the oven, uncovered, for about 20 minutes.

VEGETABLE HOTPOT

Vegetable stock cubes are now becoming easier to obtain in supermarkets and delicatessens. Shops with kosher departments are likely to stock them, but if you still find them difficult to obtain, simply save the water from cooking vegetables. After straining, boil it until reduced, then store it in the refrigerator as you would meat stock.

THREE BEAN VEGETABLE CURRY

2.25* £ 308 cals

* plus overnight soaking
Serves 6

125 g (4 oz) dried red kidney beans,
    soaked in cold water overnight
125 g (4 oz) dried soya beans,
    soaked in cold water overnight
125 g (4 oz) dried black beans,
    soaked in cold water overnight
700 g (1½ lb) cauliflower
1 medium onion
½ green pepper, cored and seeded
450 g (1 lb) courgettes, trimmed
1 small piece of fresh root ginger
30 ml (2 tbsp) vegetable oil
125 g (4 oz) button mushrooms
30 ml (2 tbsp) plain flour
10 ml (2 tsp) granulated sugar
20 ml (4 tsp) ground coriander
10 ml (2 tsp) ground cumin
5 ml (1 tsp) turmeric
2.5 ml (½ tsp) chilli powder
15 ml (1 tbsp) tomato purée
900 ml (1½ pints) vegetable or
    chicken stock
salt and freshly ground pepper

1 Drain the soaked beans and rinse well under cold running water. Put the kidney beans in a large saucepan, cover with plenty of fresh cold water and bring slowly to the boil.

2 Skim off any scum with a slotted spoon, then boil rapidly for 10 minutes. Add the soya beans, half cover the pan with a lid and simmer for 30 minutes. Add the black beans and continue cooking for 1 hour, topping up with more boiling water as necessary, or until all the beans are tender.

3 Meanwhile, trim the cauliflower and divide into small florets. Skin the onion and slice thinly with the green pepper. Slice the courgettes thickly. Peel the root ginger and then crush or chop it finely.

4 Heat the oil in a large saucepan, add the onion and pepper and fry gently for 5–10 minutes until lightly browned. Stir in the whole mushrooms and the sliced courgettes and cook for a further 5 minutes.

5 Stir in the ginger, flour, sugar, coriander, cumin, turmeric, chilli powder and tomato purée. Cook gently, stirring, for 1–2 minutes, then gradually blend in the stock.

6 Drain the beans and add to the pan with the cauliflower. Bring to the boil, add salt and pepper to taste, then lower the heat, cover and simmer for about 20 minutes until the vegetables are tender. Serve hot.

COUSCOUS *(NORTH AFRICAN SPICY VEGETABLE STEW)*

`3.15*` 🥘 🥘 `620 cals`

* plus overnight soaking

Serves 6

450 g (1 lb) couscous
450 ml ($\frac{3}{4}$ pint) tepid water
4 courgettes, trimmed and cut into 1 cm ($\frac{1}{2}$ inch) slices
1 red pepper, cored, seeded and diced
1 green pepper, cored, seeded and diced
2 onions, skinned and diced
2 carrots, peeled and diced
225 g (8 oz) turnips, peeled and diced
1 small cauliflower, cut into small florets
4 large tomatoes, skinned and chopped
2 garlic cloves, skinned and crushed

1.1 litres (2 pints) vegetable stock
salt and freshly ground pepper
225 g (8 oz) chick peas, soaked overnight, then drained
25 g (1 oz) blanched almonds
5 ml (1 tsp) ground turmeric
10 ml (2 tsp) paprika
2.5 ml ($\frac{1}{2}$ tsp) ground coriander
75 g (3 oz) butter, melted
100 g (4 oz) dried apricots, soaked overnight

1 Place the couscous in a large bowl with the water and leave to soak for 1 hour.

2 Place the prepared vegetables in a large saucepan with the garlic, stock, pepper to taste, chick peas, almonds and spices. Bring to the boil, cover and simmer for 30 minutes.

3 Drain the couscous grains and place them in a steamer over the saucepan of vegetables. Cover and continue cooking for a further 40 minutes, then remove steamer and cover saucepan.

4 Place the couscous in a large mixing bowl. Beat the butter into the couscous with 50 ml (2 fl oz) lightly salted water. Leave for 15 minutes.

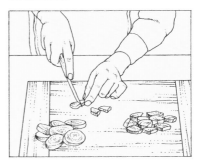

5 Drain and quarter the apricots, add them to the vegetables and simmer for 15 minutes. Stir the couscous well to remove any lumps and return it to the steamer over the simmering vegetables for 20 minutes, covered.

6 Season the vegetables. Serve vegetables and couscous on a warmed serving dish.

STUFFED CABBAGE

| 2.00 | 🍴 | f | 205 cals |

Serves 4

8–10 large cabbage leaves, trimmed

30 ml (2 tbsp) vegetable oil

2 onions, skinned and finely chopped

100 g (4 oz) mushrooms, chopped

50 g (2 oz) long grain rice

450 ml ($\frac{3}{4}$ pint) vegetable or chicken stock

397 g (14 oz) can tomatoes

5 ml (1 tsp) Worcestershire sauce

2.5 ml ($\frac{1}{2}$ tsp) dried basil

salt and freshly ground pepper

50 g (2 oz) hazelnuts, skinned and chopped

1 Blanch the cabbage leaves in boiling water for 3–4 minutes. Drain thoroughly.

2 Heat 15 ml (1 tbsp) of the oil in a frying pan and fry half the onions with the mushrooms for 5 minutes until browned. Add the rice and stir well.

3 Add 300 ml ($\frac{1}{2}$ pint) of the stock to the rice. Cover and cook for about 15 minutes until the rice is tender and the stock has been absorbed.

4 Meanwhile make a tomato sauce. Heat the remaining oil in a pan and fry the remaining onion for about 5 minutes until golden. Add the tomatoes, remaining stock, Worcestershire sauce, basil and seasoning. Bring to the boil, stirring, and simmer for 8 minutes. Blend until smooth.

5 Stir the hazelnuts into the rice with seasoning to taste, then remove from the heat.

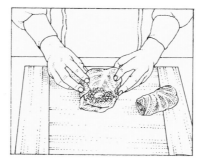

6 Divide the rice mixture between the cabbage leaves and roll up to make neat parcels.

7 Arrange the cabbage parcels in an ovenproof dish. Pour over the tomato sauce.

8 Cover and cook in the oven at 180°C (350°F) mark 4 for about 1 hour until tender.

STUFFED PEPPERS

| 1.15 | 🍴 | 288 cals |

Serves 6

3 green peppers

3 red peppers

50 g (2 oz) butter

1 onion, skinned and finely chopped

100 g (4 oz) long grain rice

450 ml (¾ pint) vegetable or chicken stock

15 ml (1 tbsp) tomato purée

100 g (4 oz) mushrooms, sliced

salt and freshly ground pepper

75 g (3 oz) pine nuts or flaked almonds, roasted and chopped

10 ml (2 tsp) soy sauce

30 ml (2 tbsp) vegetable oil

4 Season well and stir in the nuts and soy sauce. Use this mixture to fill the peppers.

5 Replace lids, then place peppers in a deep ovenproof dish and pour over the oil. Cover and cook in the oven at 190°C (375°F) mark 5 for 30 minutes until tender.

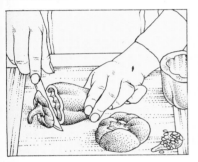

1 Cut a 2.5 cm (1 inch) lid from the stem end of the peppers. Scoop out the seeds and membrane. Blanch the shells and lids in boiling water for about 2 minutes. Drain and cool.

2 Melt the butter in a saucepan and gently fry the onion for 5 minutes until softened. Stir in the rice and cook for 1–2 minutes.

3 Add the stock, tomato purée and mushrooms. Bring to the boil and simmer for 13–15 minutes until the rice is tender and all the stock absorbed.

WINTER CABBAGE AND CAULIFLOWER SALAD

0.25*	£	480 cals

* plus about 1 hour chilling

Serves 4

225 g (8 oz) hard white cabbage

225 g (8 oz) cauliflower florets

2 large carrots, peeled

75 g (3 oz) mixed shelled nuts,
   roughly chopped

50 g (2 oz) raisins

60 ml (4 tbsp) chopped fresh
   parsley or coriander

90 ml (6 tbsp) mayonnaise

90 ml (6 tbsp) soured cream or
   natural yogurt

10 ml (2 tsp) French mustard

30 ml (2 tbsp) olive or vegetable oil

juice of $\frac{1}{2}$ lemon

salt and freshly ground pepper

3 red-skinned eating apples

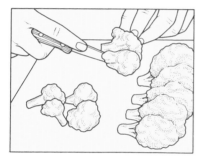

1 Shred the cabbage finely with
a sharp knife and place in a
large bowl. Divide the cauliflower
florets into small sprigs and add to
the cabbage. Mix the vegetables
gently with your hands.

2 Grate the carrots into the
bowl, then add the nuts,
raisins and parsley. Mix the
vegetables together again until
evenly combined.

3 Put the remaining ingredients
except the apples in a jug.
Whisk well to combine, then pour
over the vegetables in the bowl
and toss well.

4 Core and chop the apples, but
do not peel them. Add to the
salad and toss again to combine
with the other ingredients. Cover
the bowl and chill the salad in the
refrigerator for about 1 hour
before serving.

WHOLEWHEAT BRAZIL SALAD

| 1.45* | £ | 356–533 cals |

* plus overnight soaking and 30 minutes cooling

Serves 4–6

| 75 g (3 oz) dried black-eyed beans, soaked in cold water overnight |
| 100 g (4 oz) wholewheat grain, soaked in cold water overnight |
| 90 ml (6 tbsp) natural yogurt |
| 30 ml (2 tbsp) olive oil |
| 45 ml (3 tbsp) lemon juice |
| 45 ml (3 tbsp) chopped fresh mint |
| salt and freshly ground pepper |
| $\frac{1}{2}$ cucumber, diced |
| 225 g (8 oz) tomatoes, skinned and roughly chopped |
| 100 g (4 oz) Cheddar cheese, grated |
| 100 g (4 oz) Brazil nuts, roughly chopped |
| lettuce leaves and mint sprigs, to garnish |

1 Drain the beans and place in a saucepan of water. Bring to the boil and simmer gently for $1\frac{1}{2}$ hours or until tender.

2 Meanwhile, drain the wholewheat and place in a saucepan of water. Bring to the boil and simmer gently for 20–25 minutes or until tender. Drain, rinse well with cold water and cool for 30 minutes. When the beans are cooked, drain and cool for 30 minutes.

3 Whisk the yogurt and olive oil together with the lemon juice, mint and seasoning to taste.

4 Put the wholewheat, beans, cucumber, tomatoes, cheese and Brazil nuts in a bowl. Pour over the dressing and mix well.

5 Line a salad bowl with lettuce leaves and pile the wholewheat salad on top. Garnish and chill.

GRAPE, WATERCRESS AND STILTON SALAD

0.20* £ £ 379 cals

* plus 1 hour chilling
Serves 4

175 g (6 oz) black grapes
1 bunch watercress
45 ml (3 tbsp) vegetable oil
15 ml (1 tbsp) lemon juice
5 ml (1 tsp) poppy seeds
pinch of caster sugar
salt and freshly ground pepper
225 g (8 oz) Stilton cheese

5 To serve, toss together the grapes, watercress, Stilton and dressing. Serve immediately.

1 Halve the grapes and remove the pips. Place in a bowl, cover and chill in the refrigerator.

2 Trim the watercress of any tough root ends. Wash thoroughly, drain and pat dry.

3 In a jug, whisk together the oil, lemon juice, poppy seeds, sugar and salt and pepper to taste.

4 Cut the rind off the Stilton and cut the cheese into 1.5 cm (¾ inch) cubes. Toss well in the prepared dressing to coat completely. Cover and chill in the refrigerator for 1 hour.

GREEK SALAD

0.20* £ 214 cals

* plus 2–3 hours or overnight chilling
Serves 4

½ large cucumber
salt and freshly ground pepper
450 g (1 lb) firm ripe tomatoes
1 medium red onion
18 black olives
125 g (4 oz) Feta cheese, cut into cubes
60 ml (4 tbsp) olive oil
15 ml (1 tbsp) lemon juice
good pinch of dried oregano

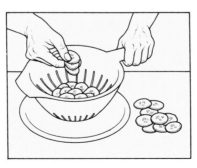

1 Peel the cucumber and slice thinly. Put into a colander or sieve, sprinkle with a little salt and leave to stand for about 15 minutes.

2 Slice the tomatoes thinly. Skin the onion and slice into thin rings. Rinse the cucumber under cold running water, drain and pat dry with absorbent kitchen paper.

3 Arrange the cucumber, tomatoes and onion in a serving dish. Scatter the olives and cubed cheese over the top.

4 In a bowl, whisk together the oil, lemon juice, oregano and salt and pepper to taste. Spoon the dressing over the salad, cover tightly with cling film and chill for 2–3 hours, or overnight. Allow to come to room temperature for 30 minutes before serving.

Sautéed Aubergines with Mustard Seeds and Yogurt

| 0.45 | £ | 135 cals |

Serves 6

3 medium-sized aubergines, about
 900 g (2 lb) total weight

60 ml (4 tbsp) ghee or vegetable oil

30 ml (2 tbsp) black mustard seeds,
 ground

2.5 ml ($\frac{1}{2}$ tsp) chilli powder

60 ml (4 tbsp) chopped fresh
 coriander

5 ml (1 tsp) salt

300 ml ($\frac{1}{2}$ pint) natural yogurt

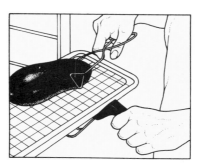

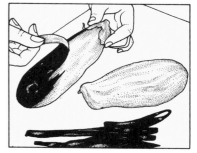

1 Put the aubergines under a preheated grill for about 15 minutes, turning occasionally. The aubergine skins should be black and charred and the flesh soft.

2 Leave the aubergines until just cool enough to handle, then peel the skins off and discard. Chop the flesh roughly.

3 Heat the ghee in a heavy-based frying pan, add the ground mustard seeds, chopped aubergine flesh and the chilli powder. Stir over moderate heat for about 5 minutes or until thoroughly hot, then add the coriander.

4 Beat the salt into the yogurt, then stir into the aubergine until evenly blended. Turn into a warmed serving dish and serve immediately.

MEXICAN RE-FRIED BEANS

0.15	173–260 cals

Serves 4–6

30 ml (2 tbsp) vegetable oil

1 medium onion, skinned and
  finely chopped

1 garlic clove, skinned and
  crushed

1 green chilli, seeded and finely
  chopped

450 g (1 lb) cooked red kidney or
  pinto beans, (or 225 g (8 oz)
  uncooked beans, soaked
  overnight and cooked as in steps
  1 and 2 of Red Kidney Bean Hot
  Pot on page 115), or two 425 g
  (15 oz) cans red kidney or pinto
  beans, drained

1 Heat the oil in a large frying
pan, add the onion and fry
gently for about 5 minutes until
soft and lightly coloured. Stir in
the garlic and chilli and cook for
1–2 minutes. Remove from heat.

2 Mash the beans in a bowl with
a potato masher. Add to the
frying pan with 150 ml (¼ pint)
water and stir well to mix.

3 Return the pan to the heat and
fry for about 5 minutes, stirring until beans resemble
porridge, adding water if
necessary. Take care that beans do
not burn. Serve hot.

MEXICAN RE-FRIED BEANS

Re-fried Beans, or *frijoles refritos*, are a popular vegetable accompaniment in Mexico. They can be re-fried, again and again, with the addition of a little more water each time.

BRAN FLOWERPOTS

`1.45*` ☐ ✳ `813 cals*`

* plus 1½ hours rising and proving, and 1 hour cooling; calories calculated per loaf

Makes 3 loaves

25 g (1 oz) fresh yeast or 15 ml (1 tbsp) dried yeast and 2.5 ml (½ tsp) honey

600 ml (1 pint) tepid water

700 g (1½ lb) plain wholewheat flour

25 g (1 oz) soya flour

7.5 ml (1½ tsp) salt

40 g (1½ oz) bran

milk or water, to glaze

cracked wheat

1 Choose 3 clean, new clay 10–12.5 cm (4–5 inch) flowerpots. Before using for the first time, grease them well and bake in a hot oven for about 30 minutes. This stops the flowerpots cracking and the loaves sticking. Leave to cool, then grease again.

2 Blend the fresh yeast with the water. If using dried yeast, dissolve the honey in the water and sprinkle over the yeast. Leave the fresh or dried yeast liquid in a warm place for about 15 minutes until frothy.

3 Mix the flours and salt in a bowl. Stir in the bran. Make a well in the centre.

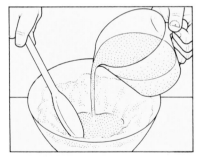

4 Pour in the yeast liquid and mix to a soft dough that leaves the bowl clean. Turn the dough on to a lightly floured surface and knead thoroughly for about 10 minutes until smooth and elastic.

5 Return the dough to the bowl, cover with a clean cloth and leave to rise in a warm place for about 45 minutes or until the dough is doubled in size.

6 Turn the dough on to a floured surface again and knead for 10 minutes.

7 Divide and shape into the 3 greased flowerpots. Cover with a clean cloth and leave to prove for 30–45 minutes until the dough has risen to the top of the flowerpots.

8 Brush the tops lightly with milk or water and sprinkle with cracked wheat. Bake in the oven at 230°C (450°F) mark 8 for 15 minutes, then reduce the oven temperature to 200°C (400°F) mark 6 and bake for a further 30–40 minutes until well risen and firm. Turn out and leave to cool on a wire rack for about 1 hour.

APRICOT OAT CRUNCHIES

0.45* ✳ 166 cals

* plus overnight soaking and 1 hour
cooling

Makes 12

75 g (3 oz) self-raising wholewheat
flour

75 g (3 oz) rolled (porridge) oats

75 g (3 oz) demerara sugar

100 g (4 oz) margarine or butter

100 g (4 oz) dried apricots, soaked
in cold water overnight

1 Lightly grease a shallow
oblong tin measuring 28 ×
18 × 3.5 cm (11 × 7 × 1½ inches).

2 Mix together the flour, oats
and sugar in a bowl. Rub in
the margarine until the mixture
resembles breadcrumbs.

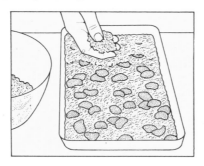

5 Sprinkle over the remaining
crumb mixture and press
down well. Bake in the oven at
180°C (350°F) mark 4 for 25
minutes until golden brown.
Leave in the tin for about 1 hour
until cold. Cut into bars to serve.

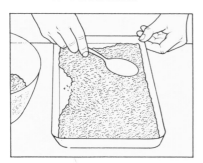

3 Spread half the mixture over
the base of the prepared tin,
pressing it down evenly.

4 Drain and chop the apricots.
Spread them over the oat mixture in the tin.

WHOLEWHEAT DATE AND BANANA BREAD WITH HAZELNUTS

| 2.00* | ✳* | 266–319 cals |

* plus cooling; freeze without honey and nut decoration

Serves 10–12

225 g (8 oz) stoned dates, roughly chopped

5 ml (1 tsp) bicarbonate of soda

300 ml ($\frac{1}{2}$ pint) milk

275 g (10 oz) self-raising wholewheat flour

100 g (4 oz) margarine or butter

75 g (3 oz) shelled hazelnuts, chopped

2 medium ripe bananas

1 egg, beaten

30 ml (2 tbsp) clear honey

1 Put the dates in a pan with the soda and milk. Bring slowly to boiling point, stirring, then remove from the heat and leave until cold.

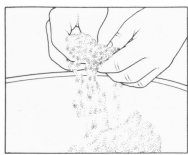

2 Put the flour in a large bowl and rub in the margarine with your fingertips. Stir in the hazelnuts, reserving 30 ml (2 tbsp) for decorating.

3 Peel and mash the bananas, then add to the flour mixture with the dates and the egg. Beat well to mix.

4 Spoon the mixture into a greased and base-lined 1 kg (2 lb) loaf tin. Bake in the oven at 180°C (350°F) mark 4 for 1–1$\frac{1}{4}$ hours until a skewer inserted in the centre comes out clean.

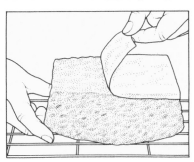

5 Leave the loaf to cool in the tin for about 5 minutes. Turn out, peel off the lining paper and place the right way up on a rack.

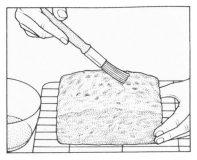

6 Heat the honey gently, then brush over the top of the loaf. Sprinkle the reserved hazelnuts on to the honey and leave until cold. Store in an airtight tin if not eating immediately.

WHOLEWHEAT DATE AND BANANA BREAD WITH HAZELNUTS

It may seem unusual to have a cake made entirely without sugar, but this is because of the high proportion of dates used in this recipe. Dates have the highest natural sugar content of all dried fruit and if used in cakes such as this one there is no need to add extra sugar.

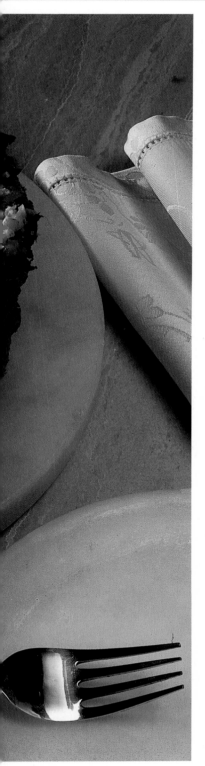

CAROB AND NUT CAKE

| 1.00* | ✳* | 591–887 cals |

* plus about 1¼ hours cooling; freeze the cake plain, without filling or topping

Serves 6–8

175 g (6 oz) margarine or butter
100 g (4 oz) soft brown sugar
4 eggs, separated
75 g (3 oz) plain wholewheat flour
25 g (1 oz) carob powder
pinch of salt
finely grated rind and juice of 1 orange
two 75 g (2.65 oz) orange-flavoured or plain carob bars
75 g (3 oz) shelled walnuts, chopped

1 Put 125 g (4 oz) of the margarine in a bowl with the sugar and beat together until light and fluffy. Beat in the egg yolks one at a time.

2 Sift together the flour, carob powder and salt, stirring in any bran left in the sieve. Fold into the creamed mixture with the orange rind and 15 ml (1 tbsp) of the orange juice.

3 Whisk the egg whites until standing in stiff peaks, then fold into the cake mixture until evenly incorporated.

4 Divide the mixture equally between 2 greased and base-lined 18 cm (7 inch) sandwich tins. Level the surface of the mixture, then bake in the oven at 180°C (350°F) mark 4 for 20 minutes or until risen and firm to the touch.

5 Leave to cool in the tins for 1–2 minutes, then turn out on to a wire rack and peel off the lining papers. Turn the cakes the right way up and leave to cool completely.

6 Make the filling and topping. Pour the remaining orange juice into a heatproof bowl standing over a pan of simmering water.

7 Break the carob bars in small pieces into the juice, then heat gently until melted. Stir to combine, then remove from the heat and beat in the remaining margarine. Leave to cool for about 10 minutes, stirring occasionally.

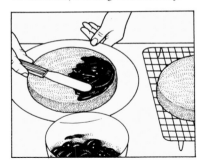

8 Spread half of the melted carob mixture over 1 of the cakes and sprinkle with half of the walnuts. Top with the remaining cake and swirl the remaining melted carob over the top. Sprinkle the remaining nuts around the edge to decorate.

LEMON MUESLI CHEESECAKE

| 0.45* | ✳* | 317 cals |

* plus at least 4 hours chilling;
freeze without decoration

Serves 6

175 g (6 oz) muesli

75 g (3 oz) margarine or butter,
   melted

3 lemons

1 sachet (scant 15 ml/1 tbsp)
   powdered gelatine

225 g (8 oz) low-fat soft cheese

150 ml ($\frac{1}{4}$ pint) natural yogurt

60 ml (4 tbsp) clear honey

2 egg whites

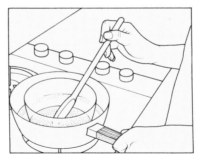

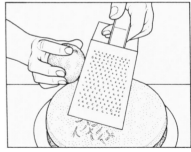

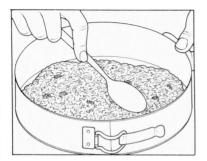

1 Mix the muesli and melted margarine together. With the back of a metal spoon, press the mixture over the base of a greased 20.5 cm (8 inch) springform cake tin. Chill in the refrigerator to set while making the filling.

2 Grate the rind of 2 of the lemons on the finest side of a conical or box grater. Set aside. Squeeze the juice from the 2 lemons and make up to 150 ml ($\frac{1}{4}$ pint) with water. Pour into a heatproof bowl.

3 Sprinkle the gelatine over the lemon juice and leave to stand for 5 minutes until spongy. Stand the bowl in a pan of hot water and heat gently, stirring occasionally, until dissolved. Remove the bowl from the water and set aside to cool slightly.

4 Whisk the cheese, yogurt and honey together in a separate bowl. Stir in the grated lemon rind and cooled gelatine until evenly incorporated.

5 Whisk the egg whites until standing in stiff peaks. Fold into the cheesecake mixture until evenly incorporated.

6 Spoon the mixture into the springform tin and level the surface. Chill in the refrigerator for at least 4 hours until set.

7 Coarsely grate the rind from the remaining lemon over the centre of the cheesecake, to decorate. Alternatively, slice the lemon thinly and arrange on top of the cheesecake. Serve chilled.

8 To serve. Remove the cheesecake from the tin and place on a serving plate.

LEMON MUESLI CHEESECAKE

If you are buying muesli specially to make the base for this cheesecake, select a sugar-free variety, or at least one that is low in sugar. Health food shops sell muesli loose by the kg (lb), and most stock a sugar-free one. Recipes for muesli vary considerably from one brand to another—most health food shops mix their own, but the majority of muesli mixtures contain rolled oats, barley or wholewheat flakes and some dried fruit such as sultanas or raisins. You can of course make up your own muesli to suit yourself, or use the recipe on page 10. The addition of chopped hazelnuts gives extra nutritional value, and would be expecially good in the base of this cheesecake. As an alternative base, you could use crushed biscuits instead of muesli. Choose a wholefood-type, which are not too sweet—ginger biscuits would go well with the flavour of lemon. Put 175 g (6 oz) biscuits in a bowl and crush them with the end of a rolling pin. Use these crumbs exactly as for the muesli in the recipe.

CRUNCHY PEARS IN CINNAMON AND HONEY WINE

1.00 | **230–344 cals**

Serves 4–6

| 60 ml (4 tbsp) white wine, vermouth or sherry |
| 60 ml (4 tbsp) clear honey |
| 5 ml (1 tsp) ground cinnamon |
| 50 g (2 oz) margarine or butter |
| 100 g (4 oz) wholewheat breadcrumbs (made from a day-old loaf) |
| 50 g (2 oz) demerara sugar |
| 4 ripe dessert pears |

1 In a jug, mix together the wine, honey and half of the cinnamon. Set aside.

2 Melt the margarine in a small pan, add the breadcrumbs, sugar and remaining cinnamon and stir together until evenly mixed. Set aside.

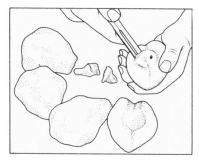

3 Peel and halve the pears. Remove the cores. Arrange the pear halves, cut side down, in a greased ovenproof dish and pour over the white wine mixture.

4 Sprinkle the pears evenly with the breadcrumb mixture and bake in the oven at 190°C (375°F) mark 5 for 40 minutes. Serve hot.

CRUNCHY PEARS IN CINNAMON AND HONEY WINE

For this recipe you can use Comice dessert pears, but be careful that they are not too ripe—Comice pears very quickly become over-ripe and bruised, and cannot be stored for any length of time. Buy them on the day you intend to cook them and check they are perfect and *just* only ripe before purchase. Conference pears are a dual-purpose pear; they are ideal for cooking and eating, so these too can be used for this recipe.

RHUBARB BROWN BETTY

| 0.55 | ✳ | 228 cals |

450 g (1 lb) rhubarb
225 g (8 oz) fresh wholewheat
   breadcrumbs
50 g (2 oz) Barbados sugar
2.5 ml ($\frac{1}{2}$ tsp) ground ginger
50 ml (2 fl oz) fresh orange juice
300 ml ($\frac{1}{2}$ pint) natural yogurt,
   to serve

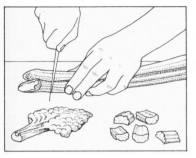

1 Trim the rhubarb and cut the
stalks into short lengths. Put in
a greased 900 ml (1$\frac{1}{2}$ pint) ovenproof dish.

2 Mix the breadcrumbs, sugar
and ground ginger together
and sprinkle over the fruit. Spoon
the orange juice over the crumbs.

3 Bake in the oven at 170°C
(325°F) mark 3 for 40 minutes
or until the fruit is soft and the
topping browned. Serve hot or
cold, with natural yogurt.

BANANA WHIPS

| 0.20 | 208 cals |

Serves 4

2 egg whites

300 ml ($\frac{1}{2}$ pint) natural set yogurt

finely grated rind and juice of $\frac{1}{2}$ orange

60 ml (4 tbsp) soft brown sugar

2 medium bananas

50 g (2 oz) crunchy breakfast cereal

1 Whisk the egg whites until standing in stiff peaks. Put the yogurt in a bowl and stir until smooth. Fold in the egg whites until evenly incorporated.

2 In a separate bowl, mix together the orange rind and juice and the sugar. Peel the bananas and slice thinly into the juice mixture. Fold gently to mix.

3 Put a layer of the yogurt mixture in the bottom of 4 individual glasses. Cover with a layer of cereal, then with a layer of the banana mixture. Repeat these 3 layers once more. Serve immediately.

STRAWBERRY CREAM

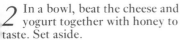 79 cals

*plus 1 hour chilling

Serves 6

100 g (4 oz) cottage cheese

150 ml ($\frac{1}{4}$ pint) natural yogurt

clear honey, to taste

700 g (1$\frac{1}{2}$ lb) fresh strawberries

1 Work the cottage cheese in a blender or food processor until smooth. Alternatively, work through a fine wire sieve by pushing with the back of a metal spoon.

2 In a bowl, beat the cheese and yogurt together with honey to taste. Set aside.

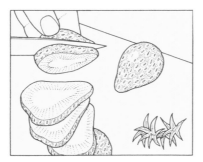

3 Hull the strawberries and slice finely, reserving 6 whole ones to decorate.

4 Divide the sliced strawberries equally between 6 individual glasses or glass serving dishes.

5 Pour the cheese mixture over the strawberries and chill in the refrigerator for about 1 hour. Serve chilled, decorated with the reserved whole strawberries.

INDEX

GOOD HOUSEKEEPING

...For the life women <u>REALLY</u> lead

Dear Reader,

We do hope you will enjoy your **Good Housekeeping** cookery book and will go on to collect the other titles available from your **BP Service Station.** Each recipe given has been double tested for success by our highly respected and unique resource, the **Good Housekeeping Institute,** so you can try new dishes with complete confidence.

It is that same confidence and trust that makes millions of women read our **Good Housekeeping** magazine each month. Colourful and glossy, it is always brimming over with new and exciting ideas, plus practical advice on a huge range of topics that affect all our everyday lives. No wonder so many people now subscribe to **Good Housekeeping** each month to ensure they don't miss a single copy.

Uniquely for BP customers we are offering a special introductory rate to all new UK subscribers of only £11.20 — *a saving of £2 on the current rate!* For this amount you will receive a copy of Good Housekeeping by post each month for 12 months.

Credit card holders can order by telephoning 0444 440421 or by post to the address below.

Happy reading!

Brian Braithwaite

Publishing Director — Good Housekeeping

Subscription enquiries and orders with payment to:
Quadrant Subscription Services, FREEPOST, Haywards Heath, West Sussex RH16 3ZA.
Offer closes 31st August 1989.

IMPORTANT: TO QUALIFY FOR YOUR DISCOUNT QUOTE "SAK" IN ALL COMMUNICATIONS.

Published by Ebury Press
Division of The National Magazine Company Ltd
Colquhoun House
27–37 Broadwick Street
London W1V 1FR

The Good Housekeeping Institute is the food and consumer research centre of
Good Housekeeping magazine.
Printed and bound in Italy by New Interlitho, S.p.a., Milan